All About Me!

Adria F. Klein

DOMINIE PRESS
Pearson Learning Group

ISBN 0-7685-1506-8

Printed in Singapore

10 11 12 VOZF 13 12 11 10 09

Dominie
Press
Pearson Learning Group

1-800-321-3106
www.pearsonlearning.com

Table of Contents

What is one?

One nose is on my face.

What else is one?

One mouth is on my face.

One tongue is in my mouth.

What is two?

Two eyes are on my face.

What else is two?

Two ears are on my head.

What else is two?

Two hands are on my arms.

Two feet are on my legs.

What is ten?

Ten fingers are on my hands.

Ten toes are on my feet.

I am Marie. I have one nose,
one mouth, one tongue,
two eyes, two ears, two hands,
two arms, two feet, two legs,
ten fingers, and ten toes.
Yippee! This is me!

Picture Glossary

arm:

head:

face:

legs:

Index